# Ozark Urchins

## RICHARD G. CRESS

# TABLE OF CONTENTS

# FOREWORD

My area of Arkansas wasn't Hope. More like hope*less*! Perhaps my worst vice at the time was smoking grapevines but I did NOT inhale! I did smoke grass a lot. There was a grass or weed called rabbit tobacco that we children dried and crumbled and smoked in pipes. I supposed that was smoking grass. But usually the "Stay Off The Grass" admonitions in my day meant don't trample the courthouse lawn. Ah, how things change.

So enclosed herein, please find true excerpts and anecdotes from my childhood and about a place called Northwest Arkansas and a society that doesn't exist anymore. Are these outrageous stories embellished? Nah! I had to de-embellish them some or you'd not believe them and I'd probably be arrested.

Have fun with this little book. Weep a little, laugh a lot, and perhaps remember them along with me. I wrote it just for you.

Richard G. Cress

One-Time Arkansas Urchin

# PROLOGUE

All of the ingredients for tragedy were present during those memorable years of 1946-1951, but our innocence shielded us from the grim reality of our circumstances. We never fully realized we were poverty-stricken, culturally disadvantaged, socially outcast, three times the size of the ideal family, and products of a broken home. We just didn't have time to consider all of that "at-risk" data since we were busy trying to survive and enjoy life at the same time.

Daddy left officially in 1949 after the ninth child was born, but we never saw him much before that anyway. He would return home often enough to keep Mom pregnant and to give us instructions about how we all ought to be doing more, and then he would leave again. He decided that his salary would support only himself and his young girlfriend and so we never got any child support payments after he divorced my mother.

Daddy left, but we stayed. We stayed together and stayed in those beautiful Ozark Mountains northwest of Winslow and southwest of Devil's Den State Park. Less than twenty miles south of Fayetteville, Arkansas, these mountains are some of the highest hills between the Alleghenies and Rockies, and are breath-takingly beautiful. Why would anyone want to leave such an Edenic spot? And besides, we had no other place to go, nor any way to get there.

So it happened that for the next five years, four boys and five girls and a slightly befuddled but extremely proud and independent mother managed to survive economically and thrive recreationally on the back side of an Ozark mountain. And we packed each day full of the things that memories are made from.

Our rented house was tiny and had no indoor plumbing. We heated and cooked with wood and did our homework by the light of kerosene lamps. We carried water from a spring, or when fortunate enough, drew water from a well. Our "one-holer" toilet was fifty yards from the house and featured a Sears Roebuck catalogue for reading and other utilitarian purposes.

We ate wild blackberries and wild strawberries and poke salad in season and crawfish from the creek and squirrels and rabbits and carrots and more carrots. On one occasion a tractor-trailer rig had overturned on Arkansas Highway 71 near Mount Gaylor and spilled a load of carrots. Many were broken and bruised and not worth reloading, so we were given all we could carry away with burlap bags. One of our neighbors had a dairy and sold cream, so he donated a certain amount of skim milk to our family. (We called it blue john in those days.) In addition, we had a 100-pound sack of flour going into that winter, so we subsisted on pancakes, carrots, carrot-pancakes, and skimmed milk until spring.

We were often cold, often hungry, often tired, but never bored. One reason was that we had each other and the other reason was that we had so many pets. The Ozark Mountains literally abounded with animals. Some were wild and we tamed them, and some were domestic and we drove them wild. This is where Shadow enters my story. Or "Shadder" as we called him then.

# CHAPTER ONE

## THE DIVING DONKEY

I'll never forget the day I met him. My older brother and I went to talk to our landlord about another matter when we saw that noble beast for the first time. He was a gelded burro or donkey if you please, and I fell in love with him at first sight because he was a potential "steed." As I stood in Mr. Kraus' yard that hot summer afternoon, I didn't see just an aged gray donkey of some five hundred pounds, nine hands high at the shoulder with floppy ears and a mangy coat. What kaleidoscoped through my mind was a fast mount from which I jousted other knights and routed Yankee cavalry and won Kentucky Derbies. My fertile imagination was fueled by every book about a horse or that used any of the same lettersof the alphabet employed in spelling "horse." I was an avid reader and an even more avid daydreamer. My reverie was broken by the sound of Mr. Kraus' voice telling Ronnie, "Yes, you boys can have him. But there is one condition. You must promise you'll never try to return him, no matter what your Mom says!"

And so it came to pass, an unsuspecting donkey changed his residence slightly and his lifestyle drastically that day. Wow! We weren't poor anymore because we weren't afoot anymore. We were now cowboys and vaqueros and Rough Riders but poor old Shadow didn't understand all that yet.

As we led him into the yard, the other seven children came from all of the place to meet him. We found we could put one teen and three smaller children on him, or four middle-sized children. Everyone took turns riding him. His gait speed was somewhat between that of a crippled turtle and a three-toed sloth. The absence of any flesh on that gaunt frame exaggerated his razor sharp backbone so that most riders would have been glad that he didn't move with any more alacrity.

Ronnie and I had seen a Johnny Mack Brown movie once in which that illustrious cowboy ran up behind his horse at full speed and placing his hands on the horse's rump, vaulted into the saddle. Well, why settle for less than the most courageous feats of other bold cowboys? The first time we tried it, however, we learned that certain anatomical facts about little boys do not lend themselves to vaulting onto the razor-sharp spine of a skinny unsaddled ass! When we *could* straighten up again, we folded several sacks of burlap together, which made for a fair saddle and a far less painful landing strip.

Shadow probably should have expired right away. We had nothing to feed him and his opportunities to graze the sparse vegetation on our rock-strewn rented place could not have afforded him much nutrition had we ever left him alone long enough to graze it. But he was fortunate enough to survive.

Some of the kids at school that autumn heard that those poor kids of "Widder Cress," as they called Mom, had a donkey. But they failed to see him as we saw him, and they laughed. (They never should have done that!) They snickered and jeered and ridiculed us and told us about their real horses and saddles and how fast their ponies ran. (They shouldn't have done that either!) Because knights and cavalry captains and vaqueros and cowboys never have taken such things lightly. And just because Ronnie was only thirteen and I a mere eight years old didn't mean that we were any less proud, no siree! So Shadow was placed in speed training. We fastened a rope halter on him and a burlap sack and cut a keen little peach tree switch and began putting him through his paces for the race we would soon stage to redeem our honor and his reputation. But our arms or switches always seemed to wear out before we could flagellate Shadow into anything that resembled "high gear." In the meantime, we had begun to brag , "We'll show 'em whose mount is the fastest in the Ozarks."

Oh, if we had only kept our mouths shut, but that was not our strong suit!

We found the answer to our quandary one day by accident. Some flies were buzzing our "racehorse in disguise" and I wanted to rid him of those pests. The weather had not gotten quite cold enough yet to kill the flies, but we had a hand sprayer with some DDT insecticide in it and Shadow needed protection from those irritating insects. Shortly, a fly landed on his neck right between those long droopy ears. I placed the fly sprayer as near the fly as possible and pushed the handle with all my might. Lo and behold, as the sprayer hissed, that sleepy burro was transformed into an equine catapult! We caught him later, exhausted and trembling, several miles down the road. Now, I didn't understand why a sibilant, hissing sound accompanied by tiny globules of moisture hitting his ears struck such terror into that donkey's heart, but who was I to question the good fortune suddenly pressed upon me. Fate had placed a motivational tool in my capable hands that would enable Shadow to astound the countryside with his speed. And we used that sprayer liberally in his training with cold water replenishing the reservoir after the insecticide was used up. Yes, we did race Shadow a few times against those brave souls who dared to put their fine steeds up against our mystery mule, but for short distances they didn't have a chance.

Ronnie was almost six feet tall so he could mount Shadow by throwing one leg over his back. I would then tie his legs together under Shadow's belly so he wouldn't get unseated when Shadow made his initial frenzied leap with the first hiss from the fly sprayer. Never sat a jockey so proud! His silks were cutoff overalls. Bare brown legs and shoeless feet dangled down to the ropes that secured them beneath this dandy donkey's gut. No traditional quirt for this valiant rider, either, only a battered fly sprayer positioned behind the ears of our aged "Man O' War." But the first hiss was all it took and Shadow screamed, "Onh-ee-oh." (We surmised later that probably meant Oh-No.) And the other horses went berserk as this dauntless, braying, lurching, donkey passed them all in the allotted space before those startled mounts even recovered their composure enough to run. I've experienced some thrilling rides since, but in retrospect, none could ever compare with the one burro stampede we engineered to perfection.

Not long ago I introduced myself to the proprietor of a coffee shop in Winslow and asked him if he remembered our family, and of course he did. But the thing he said he remembered the best was the *great* trick we performed on our dauntless donkey. It went like this: In those days the local inhabitants swam in a deep hole in a creek called Slicker Park. To the west of the swimming hole was a bluff, and next to the bluff was famous Arkansas Highway 71. Tourists would often stop on the bluff and ogle the natives and the sun-blistered mountain kids who swam in the creek. They were amazed to see the kids jump from the high diving board and perform all the other marine tricks that Ozark mountain children learned so young.

The high diving board was a huge plank cut by a local sawmill and wedged under a rock on the edge of the bluff. It jutted out over the deep hole. Well, after so long a time, we tired of playing water tag and jumping off of the diving board backward, and all of the ordinary feats. So one day we thought of an innovation. Why not ride Shadow off the diving board? Now if you've never attempted to do something like this, you can't imagine all of the logistical problems you face in physically situating a donkey onto a fourteen inch wide diving board. Shadow took one look at our proposed project, laid his ears back, leaned back on his haunches, and said 'no' in donkey language. So we led him away, blindfolded him and led him right back to the bluff. Ronnie mounted him and I stood behind until we got him onto the board and then twisting Shadow's tail, I gave one final shove. (I was considerate enough to remove the blindfold before the dive.) Some tourists standing on the bluff above the swimming hole were pointing and yelling. I'll never forget those funny Yankee accents and the man saying, "My heavens Myrtle, those kids are going to ride that mule off the diving board."

Despite their screams and warnings, we proceeded. When Shadow felt himself falling through space, he became terribly animated and vocal. I don't know if he ever learned to hold his breath or not, but he really made a big splash when he hit and would always swim for shore post-haste as soon as he surfaced. Poor donkey, he never learned to like that trick!

We eventually sold Shadow of course, because when you were as poor as we were, you sell everything sooner or later. Sometimes more than once! A stranger stopped Ronnie as he was riding Shadow along Highway 71 one day and offered him the fabulous sum of thirteen dollars for that magnificent animal. Ronnie accepted and rode Shadow the ten miles to Brentwood for the man, who in turn drove Ronnie back home. We took the news in stride for all of our lives we had been told that we couldn't keep things like the rich folk; therefore, we didn't really expect too much. Inwardly however, we all mourned, even though we knew the thirteen dollars would buy some much-needed clothing.

Speaking of clothes, we really did need them to start to school. We wore "hand-me-downs" and the child just senior to me was a girl. Bonnie at eleven had outgrown her girl's blue jeans, and I didn't own a pair of decent britches to start school. Kids today wouldn't understand my dilemma, but in the forties, girl's jeans and boy's jeans didn't faintly resemble – the girl's jeans were made of thinner material, had red threaded seams, and zipped on the side. How would you have liked to have been the one little eight-year-old boy who had to pull his britches down to potty in the big six-hole outdoor public school toilet? Counselors today might say such an experience could be psychologically damaging. Well I have news for those guys. It was far worse than that. I did attempt to hide the side zipper as long as possible by wearing my shirt on the outside of my britches.

Anyway, we spent the thirteen dollars the first week, and the second week Shadow broke his rope and came home. (He was probably bored.) We took him back to his new home, but he came right back. Finally, the new owner gave up and told us Shadow belonged to us. Of course, we couldn't return the thirteen dollars, but the man was very understanding. We retained Shadow for a while longer, but not having any way to feed him that winter, we finally sold him again– this time for ten dollars. The new owner lived far away, and we never saw Shadow again. Except, of course, in our minds and hearts where he will always live and graze green pastures and trot down dusty roads with little suntanned blue-eyed urchins bouncing on his bony back and teaching him tricks that no other donkey was ever privileged to learn.

# CHAPTER TWO

## OZARK OUTHOUSES

One piece of Ozark architecture that captures your imagination is the old-fashioned outhouse. This elegant structure has been called a toilet, john, one-holer, etc. Some of the fancier ones had half-moon vent holes cut in the sides near the roofs, and this became a trademark of a good john.

We used Sears Roebuck catalogues for toilet paper. We tried to make them last until the next edition was published, otherwise you had to resort to corncobs. We had red corncobs and white corncobs. The red ones were to use and the white one were to see if you needed to use another red one! We attempted to control odor and flies by sprinkling hydrated lime in the pit.

The Winslow Public School had a really nice outdoor toilet. It was a giant six-holer with a separate urinal. (At least in the men's toilet.) It was about one hundred yards from the classrooms. Since it was a public facility, the principal contracted with a sanitation company to fumigate and deodorize it annually. We had all been warned that fumigation left some really volatile fumes for several hours and we weren't to linger there when we went to use that facility. However, that piece of information must have escaped the attention of one of the seventh-grade boys. Having a nicotine addiction, he asked to leave class and go to the restroom. He said, "It is an emergency!"

He had no idea what a prophet he really was.

When we heard the explosion, we stampeded out onto the playground without the benefit of a fire drill. There sat the young man, still on the commode, dazed and scorched, but the walls and roof were gone, all the results of one cigarette butt dropped alongside one human butt. When the student returned to school, he was an approximation of an Egyptian mummy with bandages galore.

Our outhouse at home was a source of teasing on the part of our cousins who lived in town, but when they came to visit, they had to use the accommodations available to them. My favorite prank was to offer to carry the lantern for them at night to accompany them to the john. Once they were inside, I turned the wooden lock and left them in there for a while. Since the toilet was a long way from the house, no one could hear their screams. I'd return sometime later and rescue them saying, "We've got to get someone to fix that old latch-it's always falling down and locking someone inside."

Since the toilet seat was cut large enough to accommodate adults, small children were taught to perch rather cautiously on the edge. We escaped any tragedy in this respect for years, but one day a neighbor girl who was babysitting us, took my little two-year-old brother to the toilet, and being rather prudish, turned him loose and stepped outside. No sooner had she done so until we heard a loud plop and a scream. He had fallen about six feet down through the toilet hole into the pit. Running to the back of the outhouse, I hurriedly opened the clean-out and retrieved Kerry, but it took hours to get him clean and sweet-smelling. We didn't want to take him inside the house until we had cleaned him, so we drew water from the well and poured bucket after bucket of water over him until we felt he was clean enough to take indoors. His color changed from the outhouse brown to cool blue after the cold water bath outdoors.

The Winslow School Board faced a dilemma each year. The school held a Halloween Carnival, and the temptation for some of the older boys to do mischief at the school was irresistible. Target number one was without a doubt, the school outhouse. Some code of chivalry still prevailed in those days because the girl's outhouse would be spared, but the boy's six-holer always got turned over. It was a large and very heavy frame structure set over a concrete waste pit so it was difficult to topple. Generally, it took four or five teenage boys leaning against it with all their strength to push it over. Since it was situated about 100 yards from the schoolhouse, it was in an unlighted area which made it possible for the boys to sneak out of the carnival festivities, and under the cover of darkness, accomplish their favorite Halloween prank each year.

But school board members are only former teenagers who have grown up and assumed the mantle respectability and reason. On this particular Halloween, they beat the boys to the toilet and carefully moved the big six-holer off its foundation and back about four feet.

Later that evening, the unsuspecting young pranksters with chuckles on their lips, and hands outstretched to find the outhouse, tumbled into a pit full of human waste.  There is no need to record that those young men didn't return to the carnival!  The next day the school board members with smug satisfaction, returned the undamaged outhouse to its' original foundation.  And furious mothers washed some filthy overalls and shirts and socks.

The toilet situation was already beginning to change some however, before we moved away.  We even heard of one family who had indoor plumbing.  But not everyone concurred that this modern trend would be good.  One uncle said, "Just don't seem sanitary to me... having your toilet on the inside of your house."

# CHAPTER THREE

## MOUNTAIN RECREATION

What did children do in that period predating television and electronic games? Let me try to reconstruct it for you. First of all, there were chores and studies to account for a large part of your time. When you heat with wood and cook with wood, and there isn't a man in the house to provide the fuel, you spend an inordinate amount of your time on the wrong end of a crosscut saw, a bucksaw, a chopping axe, or a splitting maul. Since the houses didn't have insulation, and you could see daylight through many of the "chinks," it took a lot of wood to keep a family in fuel.

But it wasn't all work. We really did play plenty of games, and those we hadn't been taught, we invented! One of our favorites consisted of riding saplings. We simply took a young tree and bent it almost to the ground with several of the larger children holding it in that position for mounting. Then after a youngster was firmly astride it with arms and legs gripping the young tree for dear life, we unleashed it.

Now there wasn't a word for astronauts in those days, but we were seasoned space travelers and had the bruises to prove it. The pent-up force of that tree really "rattled your cage" when it was released. Sometimes, it shook you loose and slung you through the air for some distance. I truly believe we invented "whiplash."

At almost any time, we also had the option of going hunting. Although we considered it recreation and great fun, there were other reasons to hunt. I would place "avoiding starvation" high on my hunting priority list. We had two dogs, both of them curs — one a shepherd-collie mix we called "Blackie," and the other a spitz variety named "Rip." Those dogs could really hunt. They had to, of course, since eating rated pretty high on *their* priority list.

I really didn't know that all dogs did not live like ours. That is, until my cousin from Long Beach, California paid us a visit in his gleaming new car and asked us to board his fat pedigreed beagle while he was living in the city. We would take care of his pet so "Tuffy" would be able to learn about rural life. As he opened his trunk and removed several cases from his car, I queried him about the contents. "Why Richard, these are cases of canned dog food. Don't you ever use the canned type for your dogs?"

I was so embarrassed that I waited to reply. It was so painful to realize you are poor, naive, and unlearned that you hide it the best you can. He asked again, "Just what kind do you use?"

I replied proudly, looking him straight in the eye, "Oh, I only use the live kind for my dogs!"

As it turned out, Blackie and Rip acquired a taste for Tuffy's canned dog food, but after it was all consumed, Tuffy learned to hunt and became quite excellent at it. He also learned to eat "live" food, since that was all there was after the canned food was all gone. He did lose lots of weight, but I'm sure he felt good at being off of canine welfare.

There was a variety of game in our hills. Some kinds are scarce and some abundant. The list includes rabbit, squirrel, deer, opossum, skunk, groundhog, badger, raccoon, muskrat, weasel, mink, coyote, wildcat, mountain lion, black bear, and of course the Arkansas razorback hog.

As you might surmise, squirrels and rabbits were the most plentiful and our dogs fared well on a diet of those creatures. So you can see that hunting was a big part of our extra-curricular activities during those years. We ate some of the wild game as well as allowing the dogs to have their share.

Among the adult male population, there was a sport called fox hunting. It consisted of a number of males taking expensive dogs into a wooded area and building a campfire, then sitting around it while their hounds chased foxes. Did you notice I didn't say "caught foxes?" At any rate, the dog owners would imbibe lots of strong coffee and other strong drinks and argue over whose dog was running at the head of the pack. As teenaged males reached a certain level of maturity, they were allowed to come to the fox hunt with their dads and uncles. The men were great and mighty hunters, although they seldom caught a fox and certainly were not about to eat one. They did however stay up all night in this great recreational endeavor. This sleeplessness was compensated for by sleeping all the next day and allowing the effects of strong coffee or whatever was in their cups to wear off.  You could often spot a fox hunter's domain during the hunting season. It would be the house where the man was sleeping on the porch or in the yard in the morning because the wife had inadvertently locked the door in the evening after her Nimrod hadn't returned.

My older brother Ronnie pestered Mom until she consented to let him go with Uncle Hobert on a foxhunt. He was ecstatic.  He was being inducted into the rites of manhood.  That evening, Ronnie was asked if it was difficult getting his mom's permission to attend the hunt and he replied, "Yes, it was. She said I could go this one time but never again since she had never known of a foxhunter amounting to anything."

The laughter was uproarious and that quote from Widder Cress got repeated up and down those Ozark valleys at foxhunts from that time forward.  My mother and her assessment of foxhunters became legendary. When we went to Winslow on Saturday mornings to buy groceries, the hunters would tip their hats to Mom and say: "Good morning, Miz Cress. We were wondering if any of your boys would like to go with us on out next hunt?"

She would just walk by with her nose tipped upward and never answer.

In the summer, we swam in the creek and caught crawdads. In Noo Yawk that is spelled "crayfish," but we didn't know that. Catching crawdads was recreation, but eating them was heavenly cuisine.

In the winter we had furious snowball fights and skated on the creek when it froze hard enough. That creek was a source of food and fun, but sometimes it was also a source of misery.

Someone had placed a two inch diameter pipe across the creek, from bank to bank, and that was our bridge. Since we had to cross it daily to get to the school bus route during school days, we became quite adept at "tightrope walking." Or so we thought. However, one wintry morning we awakened to find it had sleeted in the night, but Mom said we had to attend school anyway. That meant crossing the creek of course, so all of us who were of school age trudged down the hill to the creek bank. The ice that had formed on the pipe during the night was so thin and clear we didn't notice it initially. Bonnie was in the lead, and we knew we were all in trouble when she screamed. Her legs flew out from under her, and she plunged into the swift, frigid water. She screamed a lot more then. To compound matters, she didn't wade to shore, but reached up with her bare wet hands to grasp the pipe and then she screamed again. In trying to wretch her hands free from the pipe she bounced every one of us loose from the pipe, and we joined her in the creek. Needless to say, there were no Cress children at school that day.

Now I don't want to give the impression that there wasn't organized recreation. The school provided that. No, I don't mean the baseball and basketball games. I mean the "other" organized recreation.

As most of you know, any new student at a rural school had to undergo some type of initiation. It was no different at Winslow. Every new boy was encouraged to play "kick the can." It was a very simple game. About a dozen tin cans were spaced in an upright position about three feet apart on the ball field. The resident heroes of the school would run at the cans and then kick one as far as possible with the students cheering from the sidelines as the can sailed downfield. Then it was time for the last can to be kicked, and the new student was invited to kick that one. Of course, all the spectators cheered and yelled their encouragement. Well, what would you have done if you were the outsider? You'd try to kick that "ole can" as far as you could and impress everyone and then you wouldn't have to fight the school bully, and maybe the girls would notice you and the other kids would play with you. So the new kid would run out on the field and kick that can with all his might and fall screaming to the ground, writhing in pain and holding his battered foot. The only consolation for the new initiate was that someday he'd be on the sidelines when some newer student was baited into kicking the only can that had been placed over the stake driven firmly into the ground.

For my cultural development, I learned sculpture and art and ceramics. Not the conventional courses, but perhaps those were the general fields. Almost everyone in my family drew and painted and two of my sisters got pretty good at it. I preferred ceramics. There were plenty of red clay banks in the Ozarks and some sources of blue and white clay. I would dig some of the clay out of the banks that were exposed by erosion and clean the dirt out of it. Then I'd spend hours molding figurines of animals and baking them in the oven. My aunt in Fayetteville donated some glaze to me, and I learned to make some pretty fair models. I sold many of these items to tourists who stopped along scenic Highway 71. Seeing my long hair and ragged jeans, they had no trouble believing they were buying native crafts.

On one occasion, our creek flooded and as it receded it left two huge blocks of black tar on the bank. I cut chunks off of the blocks and warmed them by the cook stove until they were pliable and then fashioned the tar into horses, cows, cowboys, dogs and cats. When I finished a piece, I then immersed the piece into the icy cold creek water and left it until it hardened again. Tourists bought all of the "tar babies" I could make.

But the recreation of choice in our area was the Saturday night tent movies held in the summer on the ball field in Winslow. For fifteen cents you could see a Lash LaRue, Johnny Mack Brown, or Roy Rogers movie. And since all those fellows rode horses, they were my heroes. I sat many times in that patched canvas emporium and fantasized of Utah and Nevada, blue roans and line-backed duns, and rescuing some blonde haired, blue-eyed daughter of a cattle baron from outlaws. Of course, the fifteen-cent admission fee presented some difficulty, but I managed to pick berries or sell my figurines often enough to cover the expenditure. But the second obstacle was more difficult to overcome, which consisted of getting permission from my oldest sister, Patricia, to ride to the movies with her and her boyfriend, J.C.

"Pat, can I go to the movies with you and Jay tonight?"

"Absolutely not, Richard. You went last week and wouldn't take the hint when I wanted you to get out of the car when we first got home."

I suppose that should have settled it, but an idea formed in my devious little mind and evolved into a plan. I'd wait until dark and hide in the floorboard of the rear seat of Jay's old DeSoto sedan and wait until he and Pat went into the tent. Then I'd slip out and watch all but the last minute of the movie and sneak back to the car and hide until we got home. When he walked Pat to the door, I'd sneak out of the car and slip in the back door.

Phase one of the plan was working. They didn't see me when they got in the car and started off to town. But as they started down that dusty rutted narrow lane with the tall weeds scraping against the side of the car, I began to lose my nerve. Suppose they discovered me and made me walk home in the dark. Perhaps I'd better let them know I was there before we got too far from the house. But if I just rose up from the back seat and said, "Here I am," that would be too embarrassing. So I jumped out from under the blanket in the back seat and let loose a blood-curdling yell. Pat almost fainted and Jay turned pale and ran off the road and sat there shaking for a long time. He kept mumbling hoarsely to Pat, "I thought I had run over that dol-durned brother of yours."

When we all regained our composure, they said I could go on to the movies with them if I'd promise never to pull that stunt again. However, Jay remained pale for a long time, and seemed a little shaky.

So it was with hunting, crawfishing, sapling-straddling, ceramics, tent movies, and reading - my spare time was fully accounted for. I don't remember ever being bored. There was recreation and fun everywhere; all you had to do was find it.

# CHAPTER FOUR

## JUST AS I WAS

Some Texans moved into our area the year I turned ten years of age.  Since they had a son my age, we became best friends at school.  They came by one week to invite us to church services in Winslow.  My mother politely declined for us, but I secretly yearned to go.  I had been once for a few minutes to a function held in a church when I was five years old.  It was some kind of vacation Bible school function.  But that was the extent of my knowledge about God and religion.  At ten years of age, I could cuss, lie, and steal watermelons, fight and play poker, but couldn't remember ever having been in a full church service.  Once before I had wanted to go, but Dad warned me that people like that, "... screamed, foamed at the mouth, shook off their clothes, and rolled down the aisles."  So we generally made fun of people who attended church.

I'm glad the new neighbors invited us before they knew much about us, or they might have backed out.  I was dying to ride in their car so before the weekend came, I cajoled until Mother finally consented to let me attend.

When Sunday morning came, I drew water out of the well, and washed up, carried in the wood and got my chores out of the way so I could go.  I put on my best clothes.  That wasn't too difficult since they were my only clothes.  The Cooks kept their word and picked me up at nine o'clock taking me with their family to a little Baptist church, perched precariously on a hill southwest of Winslow.  My Sunday school teacher captivated me with her very first story and by the time the worship service was completed, I had heard a brand new vocabulary of words, and wanted them all defined. Words like: salvation, sin, justification, redemption, hell, heaven, repentance, ad infinitum. No one ever had to invite me again! I rode with anyone going that way, or I walked, or probably would have crawled to get back every time the doors were opened. I wanted to know more about this Jesus fellow.

When I arrived home from the first visit, my brothers and sisters asked me all about it. My answer was, "It is about something called conversion, which is like turning over a new leaf!"

So much for theological sophistication!

The singing created somewhat of a problem for me. I noticed all the extra words on different lines but I just ignored them for a while, and belted out the hymns with lots of gusto. Finally, one sweet lady took me aside and explained that it wasn't necessary to try to sing all of the words on every line of the chorus at the same time.

"Those are parts, Richard, so you just learn to sing this melody and let someone else sing the other words."

Whew, was I relieved that I didn't have to try to crowd them all in.

You might wonder why a chapter like this is included, yet God became such a real force in my life that it seemed in every event that transpired from that day onward, I encountered Him.

Most of our preachers were students from the University of Arkansas, just twenty-two miles away at Fayetteville. Some were good speakers, some were bad speakers, and some were unforgettable. But they all gave dramatic altar calls week after week, and my uneasiness grew commensurate with my knowledge of the gospel. They talked about hell and judgment and what happened to sinners who died unsaved. One Sunday the preacher talked about a man who had procrastinated about his decision to become a Christian and who died in an auto accident the next week.

I sweated it out Monday and Tuesday, but Wednesday evening my conviction and fear was unbearable. Wild horses couldn't have kept me away from services that night. This was the time I would make my public profession of faith in Christ and join the believers. But when I got to the services, I noticed that the minister's automobile wasn't there. He couldn't come for some reason so one of the deacons came instead and decided we'd just have singing practice. I was crushed. I had no intentions of going through another day of dread and apprehension. Accosting the deacon, I said, "Brother Hadley, I want to get saved tonight!"

He flinched. He blanched. Stuttering he said, "The preacher isn't here, Richard. You'd better wait until

Sunday.  I'm not sure just what to do."

My reply was, "Sir, I've watched everything that has happened in this congregation for the last six months.  I know how you do it.  Simply get everyone up there in the choir and sing three stanzas of "Just As I Am."  Then on the fourth one, I'll walk up from the back pew and kneel at the altar and ask God to save me.  So we did it that way! Brother Hadley did and the choir did, and I did, and God did!

Many times over the years I've marveled at the grace of God that would meet a human on whatever level that person sought Him, and understood Him.  And since I sought Him with all of my heart that day, I found Him, and He has never left me.  He reached down and saved me, 'just as I was!'

# CHAPTER FIVE

## CONFESSION TIME
## (PEOPLE I'VE SLEPT WITH!)

Any story that sells in today's market has to have a "seamy side." And this one has just that. The underside of the "feather ticks" that we slept on had a large uncomfortable "seam." And since we turned this faux mattress each day, we slept on the seamy side every other night.

I remember well our sleeping arrangements at the "poor place" as we called it. There were still seven of us left at home so Mother and the three youngest children slept in Mom's bed, and the four older kids slept in the other bed. To allow for more room, we positioned two at each end of the bed. I always felt like I spent an inordinate amount of my nights dodging a foot to the face. We huddled and snuggled a lot during the winter. We did so for warmth. And in retrospect I think we did because Daddy left, and feeling so alone and hurt, we needed comfort and reassurance. Larry, two years my junior, really needed the warmth. He had an acute lung disease. So we took turns snuggling with him to keep him warm while he coughed his nights away, his frail body racked with pain. He subsequently died, and I still miss little brother to this day.

There is an unscientific study I've prepared that states if four youngsters sleep in one bed, the incidence of bedwetting increases four hundred percent. Or to state it conversely, there is almost no chance of waking up dry! I bet you'd turn the mattress each day too! Oh well, after a while you sort of expect it and stop threatening and vilifying those who engage in this antisocial activity and just hope they outgrow the enuresis problem prior to marriage or military service.

I'm convinced that there is a psychological pattern to bedwetting. Actually, I encountered it in a grief-counseling booklet, but it sure fits the situation. The stages go like this:

1.    **Shock** - That's what you feel when the warm urine seeps under your somnambulistic body.

2.    **Denial** - "I did not pee in the bed last night. She did it and I rolled over in it — that's why I am wet."

3.    **Anger** - "Darn your rotten little hide. Why didn't you get up and use the pot? I don't have enough time to draw well water and heat it to bathe before school."

4.    **Loneliness** - A feeling shared by lepers, people who vote for some Arkansas politicians, axe-murderers, and bed-wetters.

5.    **Withdrawal** - Other siblings vacate your side of the bed.

6.    **Grief** - An indescribable feeling of pain sometimes enunciated as, "Good grief, you did it again!"

7.    **Guilt** - That awful feeling you experience when you are the bed wetter, compounded by the guilt you feel for lying about it and blaming it on your smaller sibling.

8.    **Depression** - The place in the mattress where

innumerable drenches have matted the feathers and flattened that area so all children in the bed roll downhill into it.

9.  **Readjustment** - That glorious time when all of you quit wetting the bed or you acquire enough capital to purchase your own bed replete with a new, clean, dry mattress.

# CHAPTER SIX

## THE PONY PRAYER

With Shadow gone, we didn't have a steed anymore. Besides, I wanted a real horse this time like everyone else my age. But when there isn't any money for food or clothing, it didn't seem my prospects of getting a horse were that good. Even if I picked poke salad and huckleberries and strawberries, my conscience wouldn't allow me to save the money for a horse when my five younger brothers and sisters needed food. The horse would have to be a miracle. So I prayed. And I prayed. And I prayed.

One cold wintry day I went out into the woods. I loved the woods. They were clean and fragrant and private. But on this particular day they were something more. They were pregnant with promise. But how could they be? Everything seemed dead. The trees had shed their leaves and appeared like dark gaunt skeletons. As I continued down the old abandoned trail, a sudden movement in the underbrush caught my eye. I almost fainted. My mind ran the gamut of every dangerous beast from mountain lion to black bear to rabid wolf. Something was going to attack me, and the underbrush was so thick I couldn't see it. Transfixed to the spot, I instinctively threw up my forearm just as the beast sprang from the thicket and fastened it's teeth over my mackinaw-clad forearm. My fear turned to amazement as the wild razorback sow couldn't even penetrate the thick coat material with her teeth, and with a pathetic grunt fell over on her side. She was too sick and weak to be dangerous. My fear turned to amazement as I realized this and then again to practicality as I ran and summoned Larry and Diane to assist me. With a rope, gunnysack, and two hours of arduous labor, we got that red, sharp-snouted hog into a stall in our barn. We posted notices in Winslow at the general store and post office but never really believed this was a wild hog, but evidently it was. No one ever came forth to claim her. If there was an owner out there, I secretly hoped he couldn't read or at least couldn't count because I really wanted that pig for my own.

For the remainder of the winter we carried water, gathered acorns, dug roots and begged table scraps to keep that pig alive. She tamed down and I would scratch her belly until she laid over on her side and uttered contented grunts. She kept getting fatter until one day she deflated... and produced eight little red piglets!

I had no problem equating this natural phenomenon with supernatural intervention and immediately claimed an answered "pony prayer." Choosing two of these piglets for myself, I began my quest for a horse.

There was a bachelor who had a large remuda of horses and mules and lived only a mile from us. Although I was only ten by then, it didn't seem strange to me to walk over to Mr. Harvey's farm and attempt to transact business. I caught him at home and blurted out, "Mr. Harvey, I've come to make a business deal with you. I have two little weanling shoats that I'll trade you for one of your horses. Take me out to your herd and let's work out a deal."

I met his stare and held it. He never said a word. He eyed me for a long time then spat a stream of tobacco juice at a nearby hound. An eternity later, he picked up a feed bucket and a rope and started toward his pasture. My heart was pounding so hard I knew he must have heard it.

Although there were at least twenty horses in the herd, I didn't have to make a choice. I named her Flicka from fifty yards away. She was a dark bay filly with black stockings, mane, and tail, and a white diamond in her forehead. She was only about thirteen hands high, and I judged she weighed around eight hundred pounds. I "mouthed" her and decided she was about twelve years old. She was mine, and I took her home with me to stay. I kept her until we eventually moved to Fort Smith, three years later.

Our trick riding days began shortly after I brought her home. If Shadow had been able to do so many significant things, then surely I could dream up some things for Flicka to perform. Just riding a horse somehow didn't seem like enough. So some trick riding evolved.

"Richard, why don't you ever do the dangerous part," Larry asked. "Ronnie rode Shadow off the diving board, and Bonnie rode the bent sapling, and I'm supposed to do the horse trick."

Well, I didn't dignify my younger brother with an

answer. It seemed apparent to me that the sibling who could think up all these exciting tricks ought to be exempt from having to risk his own neck carrying them out. Surely it ought to be understood by now that I was in charge of policy and not operations!

So we prepared for the "horse trick." I mounted Flicka bareback and rode her to one end of the pasture and turned her about. Larry was standing in the middle of the pasture. With a wild whoop and a kick of my bare feet in her ribs, Flicka was stampeded into a beeline for Larry. I held my right arm out rigid and horizontal and my right leg stiff with my foot pointed outward. Just before running Larry down, I reined Flicka left just enough to avoid trampling Larry who threw both arms up to catch my outstretched arm. His near foot connected with my right foot, and he swung up behind me on the flying filly. As we neared the end of the pasture, we circled back around to head across the field again. Placing both his hands on my shoulders, Larry then stood up and as we made another pass around our verdant coliseum, he grasped my hair firmly and mounted my shoulders.

Larry never fell doing this trick, and I only fell off Flicka once. There's no telling what we could have done if we'd had the money to buy a saddle. On the other hand, there's no telling what we'd been restrained from doing if Mom had ever seen us perform.

# CHAPTER SEVEN

## WELLS & WASHDAYS

The water in those Ozark Mountains simply has to be the best in the world. Cold, clear, pure, and delicious; it is the kind of water that you'll always remember. However, the logistics of obtaining it left a lot to be desired during those memorable years in question since you had to carry it from a spring or draw it up from a well with a rope and pulley in galvanized buckets.

Our first residence in Winslow boasted a pretty fair well. It was hand-dug and about sixty feet deep and was able to supply all the water our large family used. Summer or winter, day or night, I was the designated water boy. Saturday was always my heaviest workload. It was bath day since my two older sisters and one older brother often had dates. Of course, back then we didn't say dating. We said they were "goin' sparkin'." At any rate I drew lots of water and carried it indoors and filled buckets and pots heating on the wood cook stove and half-filled a large washtub on the floor with cold water. The heated water was added until it was just right and the baths ensued according to seniority. After three or four people bathed, the wash water was emptied and the process began again until everyone was clean. Since I was water boy, I was always last, but I made sure I started with clean water. It was one of the "perks" of my job.

I had noticed a curious phenomenon on bath days. When bathing the youngsters, despite water being sloshed over the tub and splashed on the floor, the water line in the tub didn't recede. Too, the water began to take on a yellowish tinge. The diuretic effect of the warm soapy water was evidently powerful. You can see why the older children always wanted to bathe first! And why I always had my private bath!

At a later residence on West Mountain near Signal Hill, we didn't have a well. There was a rocked-in spring about one hundred and fifty yards from the house. The water was so heavy and the distance so far, that although I was only ten years old by then, I always carried two buckets at a time... one in each hand. I didn't want one of my arms to grow longer than the other one.

There were water frogs in the spring. Sometimes in summer, after work was done, I would spend an hour or so lying in the grass beside the spring and feeling the damp coolness of the mossy rocks against my hands. In time, I taught two of the frogs not to be afraid of me, and I could pick them up and hold them. Those were idyllic moments in my boyhood.

On washdays, the water was carried and heated as it had been for bath days. In the summer, Mom had me build a fire under a huge black kettle. After the water heated, lye soap was shaved off of a bar into the kettle. Then the stir stick was used to punch clothes down into the hot, soapy liquid. After a while, we'd use the same smooth, clean stick to lift the garments from the cauldron into the warm rinse water in a #3 washtub.

Then the fun part began - wringing the excess water out of the clothes. Mother would fish a pair of jeans out of the rinse water and flip the legs to me.  She'd retain the end of the pants with the waist, then she'd twist one way, and I'd twist the other direction until all the excess water was squeezed out.  Afterwards, we'd hang the clothes on a line, fence, or tree limb until they were completely dry.

Thank God we only had about two changes of clothing per family member!

# CHAPTER EIGHT

## NURSES &
## COSMETOLOGISTS

Almost all our toys were hand-made. When you haven't any money, you can get to be very creative and improvisational. I made toy horses out of corn stalks, and Larry made whistles from hickory wood, and Diane and Sandy made their own doll clothes. By now, there were five siblings that were younger than me. Kerry was just a month old, Linda was 3, Sandy was 5, Diane 7, Larry 9, and I was 11. On one occasion our aunt from Fayetteville brought us real "store-bought" toys. Sandy received the best one… a little plastic nurse kit. It was white with an official looking red cross on the lid and contained small bottles of candy pills, a stethoscope, a nurse's cap, and a small hot water bottle with a tube.

Sandy was inspired by the kit. While only five, she was extremely precocious. Her cotton-colored hair and soft blue eyes belied her curiosity and diligence. (In other words, she was nosy and stubborn!) She followed adults around and listened intently to their conversations and logged all the medical information available so she could be a good nurse. She didn't always get it right, however. Like the one time when she heard about a serious case of T.B. Later that evening, she brought her little bedraggled doll into the front room and sadly announced the doll's demise. It had succumbed to one of those initialed diseases. She didn't know about V.D. and couldn't remember T.B., so she finally determined that the cause of death was B.O.!

Our family wasn't much for avoiding delicate subjects, and this gave rise to a unique incident in medical history.  You might call it a catastrophe.

Mother and one of her friends had been discussing constipation and remedial options associated therewith, and Sandy had eavesdropped on this earthly conversation.  Later, when we were all in the living room, Mom missed Sandy, but Larry said she was in the back room playing with the cat.  Moments later, we heard an anguished yowl, a concurrent scream, and a wild-eyed cat shot out of the bedroom.  The cat jarred the screen door open with the impact of its body, and ran spitting and yowling into the night.

An elfin wide-eyed nurse hesitantly entered the living room with scratches across her arms.  She needed a nurse too, with iodine and bandages for her scratches.  After the commotion subsided, the story unfolded.  A great medical discovery was made by this intrepid medical researcher.  Sleeping felines will react to icy creek water being introduced as an enema into their rectums by cold plastic tubes attached to a tiny nurse's hot water bottle, even if the solicitous youthful nurse is assuring them that this is necessary to relive their imaginary constipation.  In fact, that cat forever avoided Sandy as though she were "Public Enema #1!"

There weren't any punk rockers in our pristine generation.  Except Sandy… accidentally.  In those days, oleo margarine didn't look like the beautiful pale yellow margarine of today.  Before instant everything was the watchword, you had to do some things for yourself.

Vegetable margarine was packed in square blocks and was white. (It was rumored that the dairy lobby required this so it wouldn't be mistaken for butter.) However, if you wanted to color it, a capsule of yellow-orange food dye was included. You could burst the capsule and knead the coloring into the margarine until it looked yellow and buttery.

One summer day, Mom was working in the garden, and Diane and Larry decided to fix Sandy's hair. Larry cut it swiftly and not too accurately as Diane prepared the tint - a capsule from the margarine. As the long tresses dropped to the floor, her weight-freed hair stood up at all angles. Diane deftly worked the yellow-orange food coloring into Sandy's once beautiful hair. The orange was dominant, and Sandy was a monstrous sight.

As Larry and Diane led Sandy outside to showcase their cosmetology skills to Mom, they soon perceived that their enthusiasm wasn't shared. Mother dropped her hoe, started striding purposely toward them with her mouth set in what we'd come to recognize as that dangerous, dangerous grim line. The dog howled and scampered under the house... the cat, already leery of Sandy, spat and climbed a tree. Our family decided this meant the world just wasn't ready for punk-rock hairstyles at that juncture in history and so it was delayed until the next generation.

# CHAPTER NINE

## RONNIE OR VERONICA

It was January, 1946 when the Cress children enrolled in Winslow schools. There were four of us who enrolled that first day: Patricia, 16; Ronnie, 13; Bonnie, 10; and I was 7. That makes two boys and two girls, right? Well, we actually introduced ourselves as three girls and one boy. Here's how it happened.

My brother Ronnie was tall, slim, curly haired and handsome. That day he combed his forelocks down into bangs, affixed a very fashionable headscarf, and looked like a girl. Especially as we added lipstick, slacks, high-heeled shoes, falsies and perfume. As we met in his office to enroll, Ronnie speaking in falsetto, explained ever so sweetly to the principal that her name was Veronica; she was a twin, and that her twin brother Ronnie would be coming to school tomorrow, but he was ill today.

The next day Ronnie came to school as a boy, but Veronica was sick now. In fact, Veronica stayed sick and never returned to school. The principal began to send notes home to Mother inquiring about Veronica, but we managed to lose the note each time. Finally, a social worker, fearing the Veronica was staying home from school because she was pregnant, went to our house to inquire about her. Imagine Mother's surprise when she learned she had an extra daughter named Veronica. Imagine the social worker's surprise when she learned Mother didn't have a daughter named Veronica. Imagine our surprise when we went to school the next day, and the principal was waiting for us!

# CHAPTER TEN

## THE FIVE HUNDRED POUND
## FIRE EXTINGUISHER

As I said previously, we cooked with wood and heated with wood. However, in the interest of honesty, I should have said that we ATTEMPTED to heat with wood. Oh, we had all the necessary items for heating with wood.

- A large wood burning stove - it weighed about five hundred pounds
- A supply of dry cordwood and green cordwood and kindling
- Matches
- Paper
- Kerosene
- And a pyromaniac (yours truly)

Well theoretically, it should have worked every time. Here's the normal scenario however. I'd jump out of bed on a wintry morning and do a staccato tap dance on the frosty floor with my bony bare feet, and move resolutely and trepidaciously toward the heating stove. The ugly monster was always cold and seldom offered any friendly fire from the last night. So I would start from scratch.

PLAN #1

Light match to paper. Throw match into ash bucket only after it sears your fingers. Paper blazes beautifully outside of stove. Place paper in stove. Place kindling gingerly on top of paper. Coax small fire to light several pieces of kindling. Place dry wood on top of kindling.

Place green wood on top of kindling.  Check stove to make sure damper is completely open.  Close stove door carefully.  Run for bed, shivering body beneath covers and place semi-frozen feet on a somnambulistic sibling for warmth.

Fifteen minutes later it is time for the entire household to arise.  Check the stove.  The fire is out.  It is a fact of life that almost all combustible materials ignited OUTSIDE a wood burning stove will die WITHIN a wood burning stove. What a great idea for a fire extinguisher!

I hear voices crying out, "Richard, you little brat. Why haven't you gotten that fire going yet?"

I switch to next sequence.

PLAN #2

Light piece of paper.  Throw paper into stove.  Pour a half-pint can full of kerosene.  Stand as far away as possible.  Throw kerosene into stove, leaping backward at the same time.

WHOOSH!  Every sibling in the house screams, "Momma, that Richard is going to set this house on fire someday if he doesn't learn how to build a fire!"

But why did I care? I had a five hundred pound fire extinguisher right there in the front room.  Only, we called it a stove.

# CHAPTER ELEVEN

## SAM, THE ARTHRITIC MULE

For the uninitiated among our urbanites I suppose I should explain the difference between a mule and donkey. It's very simple. If you breed a donkey (male ass, generally) to a female horse, you produce a mule. Mules cannot produce offspring because they are a hybrid of this breeding method. Or, if I were writing this as a romance fiction I would say that some handsome jackass wooed and won the heart of some cute little filly and produced an offspring.    That's uniformly true whether you're talking about equines or humans.

Donkeys are the smaller animals of course, and are characterized by their stubbornness, perverseness, treachery and cunning.  Horses, on the other hand, are larger, stronger and faster.  Thus it is, that offspring of this union is an animal that is stubborn, perverse, treacherous, and cunning, and large enough, strong enough and swift enough to use all of the above against you.  That is a mule!

Our neighbors had a mule.  His name was Sam, and he walked with a decided limp. Arthritis, they said. Since at that time we didn't have a draft (work) horse of any kind, the neighbors boarded Sam with us and we used him for plowing. I plowed my very first furrow at age 11 with Sam pulling the plow. We were a match. A skinny, tow-headed blue-eyed urchin behind a scrawny, braying, lurching mule.   The line harness creaked as I yelled, "Giddap" and slapped the lines tied together behind my back. "To the right a little, Sam" was in response to the command, "Gee."  If I needed him to move to the left, I said, "Haw."

On and on, row after row, we broke the ground and then laid off the rows for a crop of corn. We had to have something to eat that year with no money and no jobs; planting a garden was extremely necessary, and Sam was necessary to the project as well.

If a stranger has passed by that day and knew nothing about farming, he would have given us a little chance of success in providing food for a family of eight at home. But hunger and deprivation are powerful incentives and we worked until we had planted corn, beans, squash, tomatoes, okra, onions, peas, watermelons and potatoes. For the short term, we put in a salad garden with lettuce, green onions, radishes and cucumbers.

And so some skinny urchins and a brave mother and a gimpy mule named Sam, learned together, worked together, stayed together and survived together. We were a strange looking bunch, but we were not quitters and you should have seen that garden! Were all my rows straight? Well, not really, but you can always get more seed into a crooked row than you can a straight one anyway!

Mother had us pick blackberries as soon as they were just ripe and they grew in wild profusion all over our farm. We managed to can six hundred quarts of berries that year and with the corn and tomatoes we canned and the potatoes we put in the barn, we had a much better second winter. We did not soon forget the winter number one with the carrots and pancakes routine so we gardened and canned with a vengeance.

Canning was a pretty hot chore since we canned when the weather was already warm and then had to keep the cook stove burning hot in order to heat the water and boil the liquids. We sterilized the jars also by boiling them and this took a lot of water and a lot of wood. The water of course was from the spring and required lots of boy-power to carry the water the requisite one hundred yards to the house. The wood did not come pre-cut so it also required lots of chopping. We didn't own a chainsaw and could not have afforded the fuel for one had we owned one. Don't "axe" me how I kept the wood supply going, I just did!

# CHAPTER TWELVE

## YOUNG LOVE

The year I turned twelve, I began to notice girls. Oh, I had been aware of the opposite sex for several years and generally fell in love with all my female school teachers, but this was different. Now my eyes followed the girls my age. And since I had recently acquired a real horse, they looked at me differently.

Periodically then, I fell madly in love with each girl in our seventh grade class. I would just die if I wasn't sure we'd grow up and marry someday and spend eternity together. I can't seem to remember any of their names however. The romance cycle went something like this: I noticed her. She noticed me. I saw her noticing me. She noticed me seeing her. We sent out emissaries. My best friend contacted her best friend and asked, "Does Susie like Richard?"

She would reply, "I can't tell you until you tell me if Richard likes Susie!"

My liaison never had to lie. Of course I liked Susie. And Jane, and Mary, and any other female from ages ten to twenty, during those junior high years.

I'd like to tell you that great, passionate, erotic love affairs grew out of those trysts, but in reality these relationships generally consisted of standing next to the current Susie in lunch line or passing a note to her in study hall. Or sometimes holding her hand on the playground.

But sometimes love is fickle. Like at Halloween. Our

school always had great Halloween parties. On one year in particular, the festivities were really special to me. I was wondrously in love. (Again.) And "she" would be at the party. This freckled, pig-tailed, femme fatale loved me more than life itself. She would listen to my deepest, darkest secrets and be loyal to death. What macho thing could I do to show her what a courageous, manly, mature boyfriend she had chosen?

One of the events that evening was a blind boxing match. Four of the seventh grade boys would enter the ring blindfolded and with one hand tied to their belts, behind their backs. The one free hand sported a sixteen ounce boxing glove. And so to impress my sweet young maiden, I volunteered. We were divided into two teams of pugilists, with my friend George, and myself boxing against two brothers. Of course, we wanted some advantage so George and I coached our dear true-loves to stand close to the ropes and whisper instructions to us... hints like: "three feet to your left then swing." Or, "Back up darling, he's coming your way." Or, "Don't hit him, he's your partner."

The big fight began. The roped off area in the auditorium was filled with people who were paying ten cents each to watch my fighting debut. Well, I got "de-butt" knocked off because sweet loyal Susie betrayed me. Our opponents had subverted the affection of our loyal ladies and bribed them to whisper to George and me at the opening bell that our flies were open! They weren't of course, but we didn't know that until later.

Have you ever tried to zip blue jeans with a blindfold over your eyes, a boxing glove on your one free hand, and two hundred giggling spectators watching?  Don't laugh, I didn't own any underwear.  I went into a crouch, covered my crotch with my hand and got my head beaten off for the three, 3-minute rounds that lasted an eternity.

I'm not sure if my head or my heart was bruised more that night.  But I think my ego was suffering the most.  To think that my one true love, Susie had betrayed me.  And especially after I had sworn to her with all my twelve years old veracity that there would never be another girl for me... just goes to show you how fickle young girls can be!  Susie wasn't her actual name however, but for the life of me, I just can't remember all of their names.

There was one romantic incident in my young life that was more memorable than the others.  If you love horses and pretty girls and you meet a young pretty girl who owns an iron-gray horse and a blonde pony- tail, you simply can't hold onto your heart.

Late in the spring semester, a young lady named Jennifer moved to our area from Arizona and was seated next to me in our seventh grade classroom.  It appeared that I'd have to fight every other boy in the class to get her for my own girlfriend, but I did and I did!  She was tanned, freckled, green-eyed and shapely and was a fantastic equestrian.  She was wealthy beyond my dreams... in other words,  she had a real saddle for her horse.  (Jennifer, if you are out there somewhere, I hope you are reading this.)  She lived about three miles down the hollow from us, but the road was closed and no one had used it for years.  Her folks used the active road that by-passed Signal Hill Road and meandered in the direction of Devil's Den State Park.

Jennifer and I talked at school and of course it was about iron grays and chestnuts and strawberry roans, and line-backed duns and buckskins and blood bays and pintos and sorrels and palominos and grullas and blacks. I never even got a chance to hold her hand although I ached to do so and was sure I'd die if I didn't get a chance to touch her, and convinced I'd die if I did.  But school ended and summer began, and there was no opportunity to see her, although in mind's eye she raced across my reverie daily on her pony, with that blonde ponytail whipping in the wind.

One hot humid Ozark summer day, I caught Flicka and bridled her with my makeshift rope bridle, jumped on her back and started down the old abandoned road.  I only intended to ride for two miles and then return.  The old road probably didn't still continue through to the main road to Devil's Den anyway.  But as I rounded that last bend, Flicka's ears pricked up and she neighed. Coming toward me riding bareback on her little gray horse was Jennifer, as though the rendezvous had been pre-determined.

We didn't say much.  We just smiled shyly at each

other, and I felt my heart would burst with joy! She finally broke the silence. "Do you want to race?" I nodded assent, and she kicked her horse in the sides, and it leaped forward and lengthened into a fast gallop. I kept Flicka reined in so Jennifer could stay ahead. (I was chivalrous!) Also I had a tremendous view of her cute, rounded, jean-clad bottom bouncing up and down on the back of her galloping pony. (I was a normal male, by the way.)

After the horses were exhausted, we let them blow, and we sat in the cool fragrant grass under the shade of a beautiful oak tree, and she informed me that she wouldn't be returning to school in the fall. Her family was moving back to Arizona and she had to come to tell me goodbye. I held her hand for a while and then as if on cue we arose and straddled our mounts and rode off in different directions... forever! It was the most glorious and yet the saddest day of my childhood, all rolled into one afternoon. I looked back once and saw her raise her hand in farewell. Evidently she was looking back also.

Incidentally, I named my middle daughter Jennifer, and you ought to see her ride a horse!

# CHAPTER THIRTEEN

## MARRIAGE BY PROXY

The year I became fourteen, my brother Ronnie had attained the magnificent age of nineteen. He also had gotten employment and had fallen in love with a beautiful red-haired girl from Stuttgart, Arkansas. Life was really treating him well!

Ronnie's job was driving a cattle truck from West Fort Smith Stockyards in Moffett, Oklahoma to Waterloo, Iowa. It was a demanding job but a good job and good jobs were hard to find and harder to retain in those days, in our area. He dared not jeopardize that job if he wanted to get married.

The wedding date was set; the invitations were sent and all arrangements were completed. The wedding day drew on and soon it was only a week away. Ronnie had the first of the week off to get his blood test and prenuptial physical out of the way and was preparing to do that very thing when his boss phoned and told him another driver was ill and Ronnie would have to take his trip for him. PANIC! In fact he needed to leave right then. What a quandary. No job, no paycheck. No paycheck, no wedding. No wedding, no honeymoon. No honeymoon, no... well you get the picture.

"Richard," he shouted, rushing out the door. "How would you like to make twenty dollars?" Stupid question. I did demand the twenty dollars in advance. In that day, twenty dollars was a small fortune. He continued, "All you have to do is accompany Donna to the doctor in Fort Smith and pose as me. Just answer all the questions like you are me and take the blood test for me and I'll still be able to get married and we will not have to postpone the wedding."

Of course, out of the loyalty to my brother... O.K., I did it for the twenty dollars, all right?

Get the picture please! Donna was nineteen and voluptuous. I was fourteen and skinny and didn't even look my age. We went to a doctor's office at Fourteenth and Grand Avenue and asked for a pre-nuptial examination. The doctor went into shock. He shouted, "You want a WHAT?" He was apparently hard of hearing because I had told him plainly that we wanted a pre-wedding physical and blood test so we could be married that weekend. When he asked me if I worked, I mustered my best low voice and squeaked out that I drove a cattle truck for a living. He cursed.

Well, as it turned, it wasn't fun and the twenty dollars wasn't too much after the ordeal I had to endure. Donna's face was as red as her hair after all the accusing glances from the doctor. I'm sure he thought she was really robbing the cradle. It would have been poetic justice had I failed the blood test, but in *those* days my conquests were all in my mind. Oh well, it seems some things never change!

# CHAPTER FOURTEEN

## HOME ON THE RANGE

Our country home was some three miles west of Winslow on Bunyard Road. It now has the ostentatious title of Washington County Road #277. However, on muddy days, we called it lots of other names. (Bleep). At any rate, after passing Signal Hill and turning east, you soon reached the place we lived.

The house had been abandoned, so we were allowed to live there for the negligible fee of paying the annual property taxes and insurance; which amounted to practically nothing... roughly what the place was worth. You could sling a cat through the cracks in the rough-cut siding and the hairs wouldn't touch. The back porch and cooking room was falling down so we moved the cook stove into the kitchen. But the area was beautiful. There were gorgeous silver maple trees and pin oaks and elms. The grass was rich and lush and so green it hurt your eyes to behold it. Two springs had been rocked in and they produced the best and sweetest water I had ever tasted.

The road past us went to one other place and then to nowhere, so it was a perfect place for ranchers and farmers to turn livestock loose in the winter to forage for grass. In those days, there was an "Open Range Stock Law." Essentially it decreed that if there was an unclaimed and unfenced clump of grass somewhere you could send your hungry horses and cows to graze it. Many were released each autumn the rounded up in the springtime. Some were taken to the National Forest and turned loose to forage. It was definitely cheaper to do that than to feed hay all winter, and the nutrient value of grass was often better.

Each winter, many horses and mules came our way and Larry and I couldn't have been more pleased about the visits. We would open the corral gate and the barn gate and fill feeders with clumps of dry grass to entice as many of these wanderers as possible into our trap. We would put gravel in a feed bucket and shake it and the animals would think it was feed and follow us willingly into our corral.

For young self-styled cowboys, it was the supreme experience. There were huge sorrel mares; great Percheron draft stallions, trim little iron-gray geldings; and everything in between. Most were workhorses and had never been ridden. But a great many lost their innocence in that corral and learned what it was to have a wild-eyed, tow-headed, bony urchin straddle their back and whoop and yell and kick them in the ribs until they emulated the wildest rodeo stock in the nation. They quickly obliged by crow-hopping and sun-fishing and stampeding to get rid of those scrawny denizens that were astride them. Some threw us, some scraped us off alongside the corral fence and one ran into a narrow door of the barn that didn't leave room for the riders. Larry very calmly reached overhead and swung off by grabbing the edge of the roof.

Larry and I liked to look over a pen full of our captive stock and take turns choosing those who appeared to be the greatest challenge. If they seemed to be unbreakable as we termed it, so much the better. We seemed to have forgotten that we weren't unbreakable!

On one occasion, several yearling steers found their way to our place. All right! Our barn had a corridor all the way through when the front and rear doors were both opened. Halfway through the barn there was a partition and a gate with an overhead two by four board spanning the gate area, some eight feet about the barn floor. While one of us would haze a steer down the corridor and through the opened gate, the other would suspend himself from that overhead joist. Then in a fair imitation of Tarzan, we would swing onto the running steer's back. Wow! I can still remember how that animal would go berserk. Was it a mountain lion that was astride it? Was it a wolf? No, just a harmless little blue-eyed, blonde-haired urchin. However, that knowledge never seemed to appease those steers very much and they bawled and bucked until the unseated us. They seemed much harder to catch the next time.

# CHAPTER FIFTEEN

## GREEN PERSIMMONS
## & WET CORNCOBS

The militant nature of young boys is sometimes sublimated by hard work. I think that was the intention of Ozark moms and dads. If the otherwise aggressive young male is kept busy hoeing corn or chopping wood, it will reduce his energy level and infringe on the time he could be involved in fist fighting and wrestling matches. However, hard work also builds muscles. Muscles make a young man think he is tougher than he is. Thinking he is tough causes him to want to test his strength against other young males. And so the cycle seems to continue despite keeping the young men busy at manual labor. Besides, there would always be an opportunity for a confrontation at a picnic, the swimming hole, or the outdoor movie. Who won these pugilistic contests was always subject to interpretation. And so, another fight often followed the first one to settle it once and for all.

There were however, certain rules of engagement that existed. You were not to pick on someone smaller than yourself. (The reasoning was that they might have a big brother or sister.) The rules also said, you shouldn't try to hurt them very much in case they would become your best friends the next day. Also, they might have a pretty sister that you might want to court later. So we were immune from drive-by shootings and drug related mayhem in that more innocent era. We fought plenty, but in the main, it didn't seem to be as serious in nature. We generally survived, even though we felt like we didn't want to at times.

Was there gang warfare among teens, you ask?

Well, sort of. It was carried out like this. You and your brother and some friends would gather piles of green persimmons. Stockpiling them behind a fallen tree, you would create your arsenal and bunker. Another group of young fellows would build a similar system. Then the battle would begin. As you would dodge into the open, hurling a persimmon at the enemy, you became a target yourself. The objective was to expose yourself for as short a time as possible or to stand up and throw then duck down again before you could be hit by the rock-hard fruit. To this day, I still get goose bumps as my body remembers the impact of a green persimmon striking my flesh. I still hear the muffled curses and screams as those persimmon missiles found the enemy. It was a terrible warfare, but it beat switchblades and small firearms! We did use the term Uzi, however. We'd say, U ZEE these welts you put on me with those green persimmons? I'm going to get even someday.

There was a variation of the battle. It called for larger caliber weaponry. Since every farm used corn for feeding cattle and hogs and chickens, there were corncobs everywhere. We found if we soaked the corncobs in the stock tank water, they became very heavy and were great ammunition and also were very accurate if you grabbed them by one end and hurled them end over end at your target. Now you really did NOT want to get hit by one of these shells. They left bruises and hurt like Hades. But we tried not to cry... too much.

I suppose that is another way things were different then. Young lads were taught not to cry. "Be tough, be a little man, suck it in, keep a stiff upper lip, don't show weakness."

That was the philosophy we heard often. But today boys are instructed. "Being a male is bad. Cry all you care to. Tell it all. What are your deepest feelings? Lie down here on my couch and tell me how you REALLY feel. Nothing is really evil. It is just a growing experience."

(Oh yeah, that green persimmon felt evil.)

How about this one. "Get in touch with your feelings."

I was in touch with my feelings. Everywhere I touched my body after engaging in corncob combat, I felt the bumps and bruises.

Years later, as I served in the U.S. Army Infantry in a combat zone, I sincerely wished I could have talked both sides into fighting with green persimmons and wet corncobs. There were two reasons. They weren't as permanent and fatal as rifles and hand grenades and artillery. And, I was already much better trained than most in hurling them.

# CHAPTER SIXTEEN

## THE MAYOR'S MEAL

There were some persons in our community who were a little concerned about mother being able to feed her brood of urchins without the assistance of a man in the home. And since there were no programs for such things back then; and since my mother would not have been even remotely interested in receiving any help, they had legitimate reasons to be concerned. But they knew they had to approach the problem tactfully, since mother's independence was legendary.

The little Baptist church some of us were attending had a Board of Deacons. The church attendance was often just forty or fifty persons, but the deacons "deaked" anyway. At one of their meetings, the chairman of deaconate (who was also the Mayor of Winslow) was asked by the board to pay us a visit and see if we had enough to eat. If not, they would try to find some way to prevail upon mother to accept some help. But sanctified security at their meeting was not perfect and word was leaked to me that the next Sunday after church the mayor-deacon would offer us a ride home after church and find a reason to stay during our lunch so he could assess our situation and bring a report back to the church about what help we needed.

Well, I told mother. Then I wished I hadn't. She put Plan A into effect. From Monday, through the next Saturday, we were put on half rations. Mother began cooking and stockpiling for Sunday. I still remember some little cupcakes she made and topped them with lemon icing. I wanted them badly. Immediately... but I feared mother's wrath and left them alone.

Sunday came and I doubt any of the Cress children heard anything said in church that day for the noise of their stomachs growling. And the great anticipation we had for the upcoming feast crowded out the more spiritual things we could have been concentrating on that day. But at last, it was time to go home and we all jumped into the mayor-deacon's fine car and went to our house.

Mother excused herself and began warming the food and settling the table while we entertained the deacon in the living room. The smells emanating from the kitchen were tantalizing and I could hardly wait. At last it was ready and mother called us in and asked our guest if he would do us the honor of dining with us. His eyes almost popped out of his head when he went to the table. There was a fried chicken, mashed potatoes and gravy, a salad, fresh green beans and the lemon cupcakes. We ate like we were starved (not too far from true) and the deacon said he couldn't remember when he had eaten such a delicious meal.

He returned to the church that evening and reported to the other three deacons that "nobody in the community ate better than Widder Cress and her young'uns."

# CHAPTER
# SEVENTEEN

## A WORKING MODEL

Mother never told us we needed to work. She never told us how to work. She just worked in our presence and we learned from her example. It's amazing how effective that can be. Incidentally, her children became good workers and took pride in that fact just as she did.

The first time I realized what a hard working mother we had was in the berry patch. I was picking berries on the row next to her. The latest baby was just a few months old and mother laid her in the shade of a beautiful oak tree on a soft quilt. The child just older than the baby was given the responsibility of staying with her and calling mother if the baby needed anything. Mother picked strawberries from rows closest in proximity to the baby. I tried to pick as many berries as Mom but just could not fill my containers as quickly as she did. Her hands literally flew over berry vines. We received six cents a quart for the berries we picked and it was our only source of cash at the time. Occasionally, when she thought I wasn't looking, mom would put a handful of berries in my containers. Mother's output would equal that of the fastest picker in the field. And that, with taking time out to nurse the baby!

Within two years Mother found a cash job. She went to work washing dishes for thirty-five cents an hour at Burn's Gables on Highway 71. She eventually learned some waitressing skills and began serving tables, which she did for the rest of her working career.

Mother was forty years old and had given birth to

nine children, seven of whom were still at home when she started public work.  She never looked for a man to support here; never looked for a hand-out; never complained; she just worked.

Her work ethic carried over to her business ethic. When Daddy left, he also left us in debt.  We owed the one local grocery store in Winslow some five hundred dollars.  Daddy could have paid that from one paycheck, since he made a lot more than that.  But he left it with us.  And as I said earlier, he sent the first month's child support and never paid it again.

We wanted to try to get someplace for a while where we could all work in order to make some money. People in our area categorically went to Kansas for wheat harvest or the Yakima Valley in Washington for the fruit harvest or California to the fertile fields of the San Joaquin Valley for agriculture labor.  But Mother said she didn't want the merchant we owed money to think we were running out on him, so she wanted to stay in the area until we had the bill liquidated.

For some time then, we lived on whatever tips Mother made and used her hourly wage to pay for rent and to liquidate the grocery bill.  She never charged anything at all and we never went into debt. Credit was not an option and we skimped and got by and learned that the best helping hand that is made is right on the end of your arm.

Of course, Mother still had cooking and canning and washing and ironing to do, as well as her public job. The oldest child at home was thirteen and she was an extremely hard worker. She helped mom a lot and that freed me to do the work of cutting wood and carrying water.

Occasionally, a boyfriend would come by to see my sister and I would challenge him to a woodcutting contest. Now these fellows were not going to be bested by an eleven-year-old boy, so they showed off for my sister and I got lots of wood stockpiled that way. I must say, I feel sorry for the youngsters of today who are bored and have nothing to do but watch television and play electronic games. I didn't play Pac-Man, I was the pack-man! And having learned that very valuable work ethic from Mother, I packed wood into the house and packed water from the well and packed every day full of useful work and tremendous fun. Thanks, Mom!

# CHAPTER EIGHTEEN

## FASHION TRENDSETTERS

I suppose most of the students at Winslow School would have been considered poor. Some of us might have been perceived as uncouth, even. But there were some who were really pitiful. I'll describe one such fellow to you.

We'll call him Joey. I'll not use his real name in case he is lurking out there somewhere now. I'd not want to hurt his feelings. I'm supersensitive, you see. Well, Joey was poooooor... and since it was difficult having enough bath water and there weren't many washing machines available, Joey was often dirty. Joey and his clothing. So here is the picture. Joey would come to school in the same clothes, day by day. And it might be sometime before he actually took a bath or changed clothes, so he improvised.

I want you to get this picture now. After his shirt got dirty and there were smudges and stains down the front from the watery soup from the cafeteria, he would... (Oh, I don't know if I can say it!) Yes, he would turn his shirt inside out and wear it the other way! Can you imagine? Isn't that about the most embarrassing situation you can envision? That meant the labels were hanging down the back of his neck, on the outside of his shirt. It gets worse. In addition to this socially unacceptable style, he was too poor to get a haircut regularly, so his hair grew longer and longer. And since he couldn't afford new shoelaces when they broke, he wore shoes with no laces. I can see him now, shirt turned inside out, label hanging on the outside, long, uncombed hair and shoes flopping loosely on his feet. How pitiful. Poor Joey, he'd never be able to be accepted into normal society and surely wouldn't be able to establish a relationship with a girl. I felt so sorry for him.

As it turns out, I wasn't a very good prophet. Joey must have done extremely well in the romance department, because I see his offspring on nearly every high school and college campus I visit. I recognize them because they dress like him!

On the other hand, I dressed very fashionably. Oh, I didn't think so at the time. For instance, my shirts were always hand-me-downs. I know my colleagues at school were always wondering where I got some of the shirts I wore. It was like they were staring at me and saying "guess." Some would think the shirt once belonged to an older sibling of mine... probably a sister! But when they stared at me I could almost see the question mark in their eyes.

But they really wondered about where I got those trousers. My cousin Tommy was quite a bit taller than me. And to make matters worse, my aunt always handed his pants down to me. To compound the problem, my legs were very short compared to my torso. Sooo... the pants I wore were often half-longer than they needed to be to fit me elsewhere. So I rolled them up as much as I could to make them look decent.

And the shoes? Well, I did wear shoes in those

days... to school and church and after it got too cold to go barefoot. But I didn't like it one bit. They tell the story about the Ozark Mountain criminals who were caught and sentenced. The executioner tied them up and tied shoes on their feet and they kicked themselves to death! Well, I felt the same way. But when the snow was on the ground, I didn't mind so much. So I wore used shoes. We had a good shoe shop in Winslow just west of the railroad tracks. The proprietor would buy or obtain used shoes and resole them, put new heels on them, stain them to their original color, and buff them until they looked brand new. This cobbler could sell you a pair of used shoes that looked as fine as any shoes that were not previously owned by anyone else, and at one-third the cost. To add to your pride of ownership, he would re-box them in a brand new shoe box.

Well, as it turns out, so many years later, I found I wasn't really out of fashion after all. I hear today's kids boasting about their name brand clothes and they sound just like mine of days gone by. For I wore "guess" whose shirts, "re-boxed" shoes and "Tommy's half-longer" trousers.

# CHAPTER NINETEEN

## HOLISTIC HEALTH MEASURES

If you lived in the Ozarks, you tried to avoid getting the croup. It was horrible if you were choking and coughing all the time. And the cure was infinitely worse. My mother would put sugar in a spoon and wet it down with kerosene. After capturing and restraining the patient, this malodorous concoction was forced down his or her throat. They either got well almost immediately, or pretended they did.

Of course, we had to deal with all the contagious maladies. Measles, mumps and whooping cough were rampant. We were told to be careful about spreading those contagious diseases. Now I pondered this question. If you only caught these sicknesses from other people, how did the first victim catch them? Hmm...

At any rate, you had to hope you didn't go back to school soon if you caught measles or had any rashes. The treatment? Lard mixed with sulphur was slathered over your body and emitted a very bad smell. No one wanted to sit next to your desk.

Now there were some patent medicines for your illnesses. There was that popular liquid called castor oil. Now you really did NOT want to ingest that elixir.

But the medicine of choice was a drink called the "hot toddy". A mixture of hot water, honey, lemon if available and whiskey. Some of the men in Winslow skipped the hot water, honey and lemon in their recipes.

# CHAPTER TWENTY

## THE P-BAR-P

I suppose imagination allows you to draw any kind of mental pictures you desire.  Perhaps that's why radio was so intriguing to those of us who lived during its heyday.  We could listen to the programs and hear the excellent sound effects and draw our own conclusions.  Pam and Jerry North probably looked differently to each one of us who heard them speak.  No other door looked or sounded like that squeaking Inner Sanctum door.  But in my mind, Bobby Benson of the B-Bar-B was just a carbon copy of myself.

We thought we had become wealthy beyond measure when we were finally able to procure a battery radio.  The sound was poor and the static was constant, but we crowded around it anyway.   We listened attentively to the great programs it aired.  And we didn't have much controversy over which channel to audit since there were only a couple we were able to receive.  Our remote consisted of five fingers attached to a scrawny wrist extended by an arm.  We didn't feel badly about leaving our recliner to change channels either, since we didn't own one and did all of our reclining on a hard, cold floor.

We set the radio on a window seat with a ground wire trailing out our living room window and securely fastened to a steel rod we have driven into the ground outside the window.  Reception was always much better after a rain so on some evenings when we were having difficulty with the reception aridity, I would be delegated to go get a bucket of water from the spring and pour it around the grounding rod. The spring was some distance away from the house and I didn't always relish going after the water. Besides, it was dark. Oh, I don't mean we didn't have an outside light... we did have one. It was called the moon.

My great scientific mind kicked into gear. Urine is mostly water. I always had to go pee before I went to bed anyway. And that spring was far away... over one hundred yards. My schooling and chores generally kept me pretty tired anyway. And what others didn't know couldn't hurt them... or more especially me. So I would take the water bucket, disappear outside, then urinate all around the steel grounding rod. My hypothesis turned out to be correct. Our radio reception improved.

One summer evening, we all had the windows open to try to catch a breeze that would help alleviate the sweltering humid Arkansas oven that we called a house, when the most horrible smell emanated from the ground outside our window where the radio was situated. My awful truth was discovered. And I was now known as the maverick from the P-Bar-P ranch. Oh, the radio reception was still good, but my reception among my siblings wasn't good at all

# CHAPTER TWENTY-ONE

## MY CHECKERED PAST

We didn't have school uniforms.  So why then did we appear to be so uniform?  Well, it primarily had to do with a marketing technique that was utilized by livestock feed companies.    Everyone  owned  livestock  and everyone bought bagged feed in one hundred pound sacks to feed their horses, cows, pigs and chickens.  And so these feed companies went directly to the decision makers in the households and since pigs and chickens were  not  allowed  to  vote,  the  housewife  was approached.  It went like this: the feed was sacked in various styles and patterns of print that was of a quality that it could be sewn into clothing.  And since most people on the farms were very poor or very frugal, this was considered to be quite a boon.  A wife would see her husband unloading the feed from his pickup truck and would give him some explicit instructions.  "Honey, don't you stack that feed anywhere it can get dirty or wet.  And make sure you open those bags carefully and don't rip them.  And by the way, I want you to make sure you get the same brand and pattern until I get enough to make all the children some new clothes."    By clothes, she meant underwear for herself, dresses for the girls and shirts for the boys.

Now  my  mother  was  not  a  seamstress  but unfortunately, someone had given her an old treadle sewing machine.  Mom's family on her paternal side was Scottish and "aye, a bit thrifty, you see."  So she sewed away anyway.  And I mean *any* way.  Those first sacks we obtained  were  red  checkered  print.   They  sure  didn't meet any tartan requirements of our family, but she sewed anyway. And we had to wear them anyway.

Please envision with me the Cress children arriving at Winslow Public School in the autumn. We were barefoot of course, saving our shoes until the weather was colder. But the girls were decked out in red checkered dresses. Sort of. And the boys had red checkered shirts. Sort of. You could hear the snickers of the kids who were affluent enough to avoid our dress code, but at least we were all uniform.

Well, there's more. The flour companies got into the act. Or maybe they were first, I simply don't remember. Their flour was bagged in thinner and softer sacking and it generally was white. This material was transformed into wash cloths (that's warsh cloths in the Ozarks), dish cloths, and yes, girls panties, a.k.a. bloomers. Thus it was, on windy days, the girls now had two reasons to try to keep the wind from hoisting their skirts. One of course was modesty and the other was this: who would want to display their panties knowing that *Yukon's Best Flour* was printed across the rear. Or how about *Pillsbury's Best*, followed by XXX. I can assure you, if Victoria had to wear such panties, they would definitely be Victoria's Secret.

# CHAPTER TWENTY-TWO

## BURIED TREASURE

I suppose everyone who has grown up poor has fantasized about having some sort of instant wealth bestowed upon them. My favorite stories were about finding an abandoned gold mine or inheriting a million dollars. I never really thought it would happen, but something quite unusual did transpire in that regard.

We had an old tool shed on the place where we were living and one section of it had been used to garage equipment. Perhaps a T-Model Ford or tractor. The dirt was soft there and one day Larry and I thought we would dig up an area that was against the south wall. Imagine our surprise when we had only excavated a foot or so of the soft dirt and heard the shovel clang against something hard. We hit the same area again and heard the metallic ring again. We got really excited then and started digging in earnest. It wasn't long until we had unearthed a metal box. As we pulled it from the hole, we could see that it was a locked box and we didn't waste much time finding a hatchet and breaking the lock off of the container. We opened the box and nearly fainted. It was absolutely full of currency. But we were disappointed to find it wasn't American greenbacks. It was Japanese currency.

"Look Mom," Larry shouted as we carried the dirty metal box into the kitchen. "We found a box full of money!"

As she hurried over to the table to inspect it, she was as puzzled as we were. How did it come to be buried there?  Bonnie came rushing into the kitchen to see what we were talking about, so we held a high level conference right then and there.  We made some rules.  First of all, we couldn't tell anyone about it.  Secondly, we would try to determine where it came from and thirdly we'd try to find a way to get the currency exchanged for U.S. dollars.  Of course, we didn't have a bank account nor any money to open one but maybe a banker would take it and do some sort of exchange for a fee.

The Korean War has just started and several fellows had told us about taking Rest and Recuperation trips to Japan.  Was it possible that one or more of those G.I.s had robbed a Japanese bank while they were there and smuggled the money back to the U.S.?  The more we considered all the possibilities the more nervous we got.  We were thinking since the place we were living at the time had been abandoned before we moved in, someone might have thought it was a pretty good place to stash the money until things cooled down.  We decided in the interest of safety, that we'd bury the box back in the same place and wait awhile.  If it really was stolen money, then it was very likely that the robber would be back to claim his money and we didn't want someone in our family killed over it.  We researched and found that at the current exchange rate it was only a few thousand dollars in our currency even though it was an entire box full of money.

With that decided, we started making a few discreet

inquiries to see if anyone knew who had lived at that location before we moved in.  Did they have anyone in their family who was in the military?  If so, had he served in the Pacific?

We didn't have to worry about the problem very long.  One day after returning home from a short trip to Fayetteville, Larry and I went out to the equipment shed and there was a fresh hole.  As we checked the spot, the metal box was gone.  We never did find out who took it.

I was hoping it would be left for me to spend.  I certainly had a *yen* for that money.

# CHAPTER TWENTY-THREE

## WINSLOW WISDOM

One of the first things I learned was that you did not meander through the forests if you were not sure you were welcome. Some of the mountaineers had large cooking vats where they brewed a commodity that they sold to certain close-mouthed customers. They were basically corn farmers but they measured their fields' output by the gallon; not by the bushel.

I remember my older brother's birthday party at which many of his friends were in attendance. One of them brought some clear liquid in a quart jar and hid it in an outbuilding. However, his younger brother and I spied on him and as soon as he went into the house we decided to test the "octane" of that clear juice. Each of us sipped a tiny amount and decided the older boys could have it. I thought if I wanted to be a flame-swallower I would join the circus and be paid for it and that fire could not be hotter than what we had just ingested.

Another tidbit of knowledge was that you did not mess with another guy's girl, unless he was considerably smaller than you. But the cuter the female, the more likely I was to develop amnesia and forget that rule. Savage fights often broke out in that regard, on our schoolyard, both during school and at some of the festivities that were often held on the premises. Those buildings and yards hosted most of the local parties.

# CHAPTER TWENTY-FOUR
## IT WASN'T EDEN

Even in Eden there was a serpent.  And despite all the beauty of those pristine lakes and beautiful verdant mountains with pure water and fresh air, there was still plenty of evil and ugliness and pests.  We had to deal with ticks, snakes, beggar lice, cockleburs, and goathead stickers.  And since we were barefoot much of the time, the problems were multiplied.

The year I was in the seventh grade, I sat in the second row of desks and three girls my age occupied desks in front of me.  They were all pregnant.  Of course none of the three were married.   The families that allowed that to happen should have been beaten.  And the men who got these girls pregnant should have been brought to trial.  In this more recent age, they would have been.  Eventually, Washington County Social Services did get involved and removed some children from the homes where these travesties occurred, but for many it was too little, too late.

There were two "houses of ill repute" in Winslow in those years.  Some of their customers were local and some were the railroaders who came into Winslow.

One of the other horrible problems that plagued our otherwise peaceful area was the violence that erupted from time to time as a result of family feuds.   One Saturday morning shotguns, axes, and pocket knives were wielded in savage attacks that erupted on the main street in Winslow.  The County Sheriff arrived quickly and ended the fight and that was the end of that feud, thank

God.  One of the warring families moved to California and that helped resolve the fighting.

# CHAPTER TWENTY-FIVE

## I FAINTLY RECOLLECT

There were a couple more incidents that my family recalls and I remember also, although rather "faintly". At age sixteen, my brother Ronnie dropped out of school for a year to work, before going back to high school the next year.  That year, on a Christmas Eve, Ronnie met with some friends at Slicker Park Café and was socializing with the Reed boys.  He had been paid his weekly wage that day and was celebrating and showing his money quite openly.  But when he had imbibed all the strawberry soda and eaten all the moon pies he could hold, he decided to walk home.  It was only a half-mile and with a full moon out, it wasn't too dark to walk so he left the café.  However, as he walked across the little concrete bridge that crossed the creek, he heard someone in the brush across the road from him.  And this I faintly recall...

It seems that Randall Reed had opened his presents early that evening.  One really nice gift was a very realistic pair of cap revolvers with belt and holsters.  His uncle Wallace asked to borrow them for a few minutes and beat Ronnie to the place where the bridge crossed the road to our house.  He startled Ronnie, as he moved from the dark cover of the brush and yelled, "This is a hold-up.  I want all your money."

Ronnie was petrified.  He threw his billfold into the road and said, "Take it all mister, just don't shoot me."


"No Son, I want to give you a fighting chance."  Then

he tossed one of the cap pistols at Ronnie's feet. Ronnie immediately fainted.

The pretend robber was alarmed then. Had he gone too far? He ran over to Ronnie and tried to revive him. He rubbed snow in his face and kept telling him it was his friend but Ronnie was still passed out. Wallace picked him up, slung him over his shoulder and carried him the rest of the way home; awakening my diminutive mother. Now get this picture: Wallace was several inches over six feet tall and weighed over 200 pounds. Mom was about five feet tall and didn't weigh 100 pounds. But mother screamed, ranted and raved as Wallace apologized and backed out of the yard.

I've asked Ronnie if he remembered the incident and he always replied that he had a "faint recollection."

The second incident happened soon after this one. My older sister Bonnie was dating Clarence Williams - a preacher. Well, that should have been tame, huh? Well, not this night. Mom often sent me along to monitor their amorous activities. My sister decided if I had a girl-friend along, I'd not pay much attention to her. So they invited Beverly Creed to be my date that evening. I was rather smitten with her although she was three years older than me. (I believe she thought of herself as a babysitter.)

I don't remember where we went that evening initially, but later we stopped at BrentLow Café where Dorothy Branson served us some "shoe soles" (a delicious pastry with confectionary sugar sprinkled over it) and our regular R.C. Colas.

I just recall that it was pretty dark as Clarence finally drove us home.  We stopped near a cemetery where a burial was scheduled for the next morning.  And so a plan evolved in the devious mind of that preacher.  He called me aside and whispered that he would crawl down into the grave and I was to walk Beverly to the edge of the hole without her being aware of where Clarence was hiding.  Bonnie was standing at the far end of the grave, chattering away so Beverly would not notice.  Then I stepped away from between her and the grave and Clarence reached up and grasped her ankle and in a spooky voice, said, "I've gotcha!  Come down here with me."  She swooned, fainted and fell.  Bonnie and Clarence immediately picked her up we put her in the car and got out of there.  I "faintly" recall how ashen she looked.

# CHAPTER TWENTY-SIX

## THE 5-H CLUB

I learned about a new club at school one day.  It was called 4-H and I was told that it stood for head, heart, hands and health.  The members could have a project of their own choosing and primarily it was of a rural sort.  Some chose to raise sheep, some goats, some calves and some foals or even piglets.  I was so excited and joined immediately and then rushed home after school to tell my mom and siblings about it.

Mother seemed contemplative and didn't answer right away.  The question was painful for her to pose, but she said, "Richard, what can you do for a project?  We have no livestock  nor  any money to buy you a lamb or calf."

I replied with all my youthful optimism, that I'd think of something.  The next day I asked the 4-H sponsor what I might have as a project if I didn't have any livestock.  As he asked questions about my options he did voice one I could answer in the affirmative.  "Richard does your mom have a tractor?"

I got very excited and said we did.  The old farm that Washington County let us live in for payment of the past taxes came with an inoperable steel-wheeled tractor sitting out in the old garden area.  There was my project.  But I knew nothing about machinery.  We had never owned an automobile and I didn't even own a father anymore.  But the next day I crawled up on that tractor and dreamed about getting it running and becoming a bona fide member of 4-H.

The next time my brother-in-law came to visit I asked him to look at it for me. His findings did not cheer me one bit. It needed a battery, the wiring system wasn't intact anymore and the motor was probably frozen up. This was devastating news to a twelve year-old boy.

Here I am sixty years later, driving my Massey Ferguson tractor across my fields, while my Ford 8N sits idle under the carport and remembering the old tractor that wouldn't run and the young boy whose 4-H dreams became 5-H. That extra H stood for hopeless. I could not then, and never did find a way to dream up a viable project to join the other youngsters in this fine organization.

But the extreme poverty of those years is just a memory as I've now been blessed with the realization of all my dreams, hopes and aspirations. They just didn't transpire when I was "Richard, the Ozark Urchin "

# EPILOGUE

As I stood there near the spring that supplied our water, and talked to the current owner of the land where these events took place some fifty years ago, I'm filled with a mixture of nostalgia, sadness and pride. Richard, the barefooted, cotton-topped urchin would like who he became... a good father, a hard-working man, a devoted husband, a fiery preacher, and a fun guy who still loves to do mischievous, outrageous things. He'd love the two saddles hanging in his barn and ponies bought for grandchildren.

And I still remember fondly, "Richard the Ozark Urchin." I liked him. I wouldn't have changed much about him. I'm proud of his hard work and sense of loyalty to his mom and younger siblings... I would have enjoyed the little scamp.

CPSIA information can be obtained
at www.ICGtesting.com
Printed in the USA
LVOW13s1011021017
550860LV00017B/400/P